It's Arbor Day,

Charlie Brown

Charles M. Schulz

Random House · New York

Library of Congress Cataloging in Publication Data

Schulz, Charles M. It's Arbor Day, Charlie Brown. SUMMARY: Charlie Brown has difficulty appreciating his friends' efforts to celebrate Arbor Day. [1. Arbor Day—Fiction. 2. Baseball—Fiction] I. Title.
PN6728.P4S322   ISBN 0-394-83447-X   ISBN 0-394-93447-4 lib. bdg.

Manufactured in the United States of America   3 4 5 6 7 8 9 0

I sure hope Miss Othmar doesn't call on me. I didn't have a chance to study the assignment on holidays.

She called on me!

What's Arbor Day? That's simple.

That's the day when all the ships come sailing into the arbor.

I've never been so humiliated in all my life! And now my teacher says I have to give a complete report on Arbor Day.

Don't worry about it, Sally. I'm sure we can find some books about Arbor Day in the library.

Oh, Linus, are *you* going to help me?

Good grief!

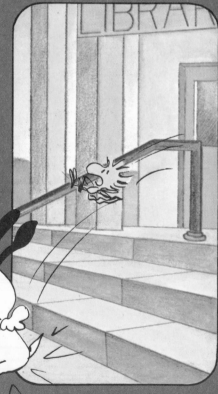

"Unlike most holidays, which fall on a particular day, Arbor Day is celebrated on different days in different states throughout the springtime months."

Isn't springtime when a young man's fancy? . . . How's your fancy, Linus?

"The first Arbor Day was April 10, 1872. Its main idea is that of conservation. Arbor Day points out to both children and adults the need to maintain and protect certain areas of our natural forests and woodlands."

Oh, Linus. You read so poetically.

"*Arbor* means 'trees.' So this is a day dedicated to trees and to their natural beauty and to their preservation...."

Linus, this gives me a wonderful idea!

Why don't we go outside and find a nice big tree and sit under it?

We can hold hands and talk and look into each other's eyes....

AAARGH!!!!

Then you can ask me to a movie, and we can sit together.

We can sip a drink from the same cup—a LOVING cup!

You know what I don't understand, Chuck? I don't understand
love. Explain love to me, Chuck.

I can recommend a
book, or a painting, or
a song, or a poem. But
I can't explain love.

Ah, come on, Chuck!
Try to explain love.

Well, say I happen
to see this cute little
girl walk by, and I . . .

Why does she have to be cute, Chuck? Huh? Can't someone fall in love with a girl who isn't cute and has freckles and a big nose? EXPLAIN THAT, CHUCK!

Well, maybe you're right. Let's just say that I happen to see this girl walk by who has a great big nose, and . . .

I DIDN'T SAY "A GREAT BIG NOSE," CHUCK!!!

You not only can't explain love. Actually, you can't even talk about it.

Well, then, let's talk about something *I* can explain–baseball. Have you seen our baseball schedule for the new season, Chuck? My team plays your team fifteen times. We slaughter you twice in April, smash you three times in May, ruin you twice in June, murder you three times in July, annihilate you four times in August, and destroy you altogether in September.

My stomach hurts.

Well, the season starts in a couple of weeks, Chuck.
Let's shake for good luck.

Thanks.

You touched my hand, Chuck,
you sly dog. I think you know
more about love than you let on.

Hey, what's going on? Where are you going with all the garden tools?

My boyfriend and I are going to prepare for Arbor Day.

I'm not your boyfriend.

"Other holidays repose upon the past. Arbor Day proposes for the future." I'm quoting from the writings of the famous J. Sterling Morton.

Who?

Mr. Morton was an early voice for conservation!

Every child should plant an orchard! A flower garden! Let us onto the fields and cultivate a few forest trees!

Not a bad idea.

Right here is a good place. There's plenty of room, a lot of dirt . . .

Hey, wait a minute. This is Charlie Brown's baseball field. There's his pitching mound. You can't plant here.

Au contraire. Here is just the place. There's lots of room. We might just as well put it to good use. I'll go back to the nursery and get some stuff. Come on, Linus, you help me.

Hello, yes, this is he, Chuck.
Uh, I mean Charlie Brown.

Just called to touch base, Chuck,
to remind you our first game will
be at your field.

We're the visiting team. I hope
your field is in great shape—even
if your team won't be. Get the
grass mowed and the infield raked,
Chuck.

Don't worry. We'll be ready. I mean
our field is ready. Well, I mean I'll check
it out.

Hi, Charlie Brown! We decided to spruce up your old ball field.

Hey, that's great! I was just talking to Peppermint Patty about that. We should mow the grass, and rake up the infield, and get everything ready for our first game.

Don't worry, Charlie Brown. It's all in good hands. We're fixing it up for you.

I think we should tell
Charlie Brown. . . .

Not to worry, Charlie Brown.

Great! Thanks a lot. I'll call
Peppermint Patty and give her
a report.

Peppermint Patty? I just wanted to report. Everything is in
good hands. Our field will be ready for the first game.

Right here will be fine.

Here? But Lucy, I don't think this
is a good idea because . . .

Just dig!

Okay, but I don't think Charlie Brown
is gonna like this.

That's perfect. It's about time
we had a little class on the pitcher's
mound.

This looks great. But I think we're
gonna need more plants and more help.
Let's get the whole team to help.

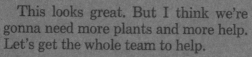

Hey, Charlie Brown, we're doing a great job. We just need a bit more help and material.

Great! I'll help too.

No, Charlie Brown. You stay put, and work out your strategy and all your plans for the season. We're gonna do this on our own.

Gee, that's real thoughtful and nice of you.

Not to worry, Charlie Brown. Not to worry.

Okay, okay, let's keep it moving. Schroeder, put those rosebushes at third base. Linus, put those geraniums at first and second. Sally, plant those daisies at home plate. Let's go, let's go, let's go!

Let's see, Peppermint Patty is their big slugger, so I'll walk her each time she comes to bat. But she might get mad.

Let's see, Snoopy's my best hitter, so I'll lead off with Snoopy. Then Schroeder, then Linus. That'll fill the bases up. I'll come up and hit a home run.

There I go, daydreaming again.

Chuck, I've got my team all fired up. We're ready.

So are we.

Even though you haven't got a chance, Chuck, we gotta play straight. I can't go easy on you, you know. Even if we get you twenty-four to nothing, and you come up to bat, I'll have to fan you, Chuck. Nothing personal, you know.

It's the only way. However, I was hoping for . . .

I'll bring my troops over, Chuck. See ya, pal!

It's the first game of the season, Charlie Brown, and we have something to tell you. In honor of all the time and effort you have given to our team, we're gonna name the baseball field Charlie Brown Field.

Gulp! Well, uh, uh, uh . . . I don't know . . . uh . . . my name! How can I . . . gulp! How can I thank you? . . .

Well . . . uh . . . maybe you . . . uh . . . ought to come see the field.

Yeah! Let's go!

There it is, Charlie Brown! Happy Arbor Day!

WHAT HAVE
YOU DONE?!!!

It was all my idea, big brother—to celebrate
Arbor Day and to make Charlie Brown Field
presentable.

But we can't play baseball here!
It's impossible! Can't you see that?

Oh, come on, Charlie Brown,
We couldn't play before anyway.
So you haven't lost anything.

Look at my pitcher's mound. It's
got a tree on it! I can't pitch from
there!

Come on, Charlie Brown, give it
a try. Beethoven never gave up.

Beethoven never had a tree on his piano.

And look at that! A scarecrow!

Peppermint Patty is going to be here any moment. What'll she think?

Hey, Chuck! Here we are! Let's get right to the game.

Hey! What's this?

Well, my team thought it would be nice, on account of Arbor Day to . . .

CHUCK! ARE YOU MAD? This is the craziest thing you've ever done! You've got everything here but cattle and sheep!

MOOOO!

Chuck! You have to be the most dumb manager that ever lived!
How can I pitch from this crazy mound with a tree on it?

Well, I'll have to make the best of it.

AAARGH!! IT WON'T WORK!!

If I hit a home run, Schroeder, will you give me a kiss?

If *you* hit a home run, I'll meet you at home plate and give you the biggest kiss you've ever had!

INCENTIVE!

No problem. She's never hit the ball out of the infield in her life.

She did it!! SHE HIT A HOME RUN!!! And you're going to have to stand out by home plate and kiss her! YOU PROMISED!!

A promise is a promise.

Forget it! If that's the only way I'll ever get you to kiss me, forget it!

Another victory for women's lib!

Okay, Chuck, you were lucky to get one run.
But now our best batters are coming up.

Can you believe it? It's already the third inning, and we're ahead! I think we're going to win our first game ever!

The only thing that could keep us from winning today would be to have the game rained out. But there's no chance of that.

There's not a cloud in the sky.

NO! We're not going to postpone!!

It's starting to rain, Charlie Brown. Aren't we going to call the game?

No, we're not going to call the game. So you might as well get back out there in center field where you belong!

Hey, where's everybody going?

QUITTERS! THAT'S WHAT YOU ARE!! YOU'RE ALL A BUNCH OF QUITTERS!

At least it's good for the crops, Charlie Brown.

BUT WE WERE WINNING! . . . WE WERE WINNING. . . .

So I'm happy to report that all our trees and plants
are doing very well.

And I'd like to complete my report by quoting J. Sterling
Morton, founder of Arbor Day. In closing his Washington
Arbor Day address of 1894 he said, "So every man, woman,
and child who plants trees shall be able to say on coming as
I come, toward the evening of life, in all sincerity and truth,
'If you seek my monument, look around you!'"

Thank you.

I'm sorry about the game being called, Chuck, I know you're sad 'cause you didn't win. But you wouldn't have wanted to win a game that way, would you, Chuck? I mean the rain and all that?

Well, maybe you're right. But I wonder if I'll ever win at anything.

Well, at least you've got a baseball field named after you, Chuck. And it's got all those pretty trees and plants.

Happy Arbor Day,
Charlie Brown!